T0107673

LOST
MEMORIES

LOST
MEMORIES

Helen Smith

iUniverse, Inc.
Bloomington

Lost Memories

iUniverse books may be ordered through booksellers or by contacting:

iUniverse
1663 Liberty Drive
Bloomington, IN 47403
www.iuniverse.com
1-800-Authors (1-800-288-4677)

ISBN: 978-1-4759-2261-5 (sc)
ISBN: 978-1-4759-2262-2 (ebk)

Printed in the United States of America

iUniverse rev. date: 05/13/2012

CONTENTS

MY DREAM

Have you ever looked into a mirror and saw nothing at all.
Have you ever gone to sleep and forgot to dream.
Have you ever walked though life and if had no meaning.
Have you ever dreamt of a man and wished he was real.

I had a dream last night that felt so real.
I felt a man that I wanted to be mine.
But in my reality could it be true.
M y dreamed that I wish to be true,
My heart pounds at the thought of that.
My mind may wonder,
But my dreams stay the same, there of you all the time.

I pray to god never to awake I'm happy where I am
Make no mistake
If dreams came true I'd take you.
You're my every thought,
You're my dreams,
You're my everything.
Stay where you are all my life
Because if you're not my heart will break
Like a piece glass hitting the floor.
My dreams will shatter make no mistake,
I love you very much
And I thank you for that.

Love Started with You

Roses are Red.
violets are Blue
My life truly Began
When I met you.
your Kisses are like a
fine wine, the elegance of
it is like your tongue.
Your Body is the Best
like the angles came down
from Heaven and made
you mine Your Heart is
made of fine gold just
like I thought. When I look
into your eyes I still turn
into goo. your all my
dreams and all my thought
rapped into a perfect
person which is you. I'm
Blessed every day that
you are there. my Heart
rejoices with each minute
we share, the days and
weeks here alone are
empty and sad and nothing
gets done. my energy
with in comes from your
love to me, I thank the Lord
for my god sends that
make me wake up each and
every morning. Thank-you
My love for all your time
We will life forever until
the end of all time xoxo.

MY KNIGHT

You are my Knight in shinning
armor, you are my savior
You are my every thought,
You are my every feeling.
You are my Life, I always
believed there is somebody
for everyone that was always
gods plan. since the beginning
of time, You go through Life
simple doing the motions,
Day to Day with nothing, at
one time I guess that was
fine, no true love, no true
connection to another
person. Your life at Birth
already Planned, your fait in
world and all its wrongs,
till that day you sleep so
Sound never to awake to the
things around the pain is
great in such things the past
has a way, the future is
their Let me know the
past is buried like it should.
the future in my life
seems like dream and my
past gets buried like it
Should you search through
your life night and Day to find
the one your with is in
perfect harmony the world
stops spinning Just for
a minute and it's done.

LOVE

I all ways thought that in order to be Happy
there was all so a major sacrifice, because
in life it can throw you some really strange
balls. But after it all I still found you to be in
my life.

In my mind of thought I would never imagine
that life could be fair but
yet you are there. And If in life you find that one
chance take
it in hand and hold on to it.

Some times in this crazy world that we live in
doesn't seem really fair, but when it is and it
Hands you that bird take it and get prepared
for your life and put your hands on every were.

This chance of a life time happens maybe once
so don't blow it and take care.

FORGIVENESS

Some times in the darkest part of our minds things
that have happened in the past come back in time.
Your mind is a very power full drug that sometimes
won't shut down.

The things we remember but try to forget because
the pain of the past is so great. The horrible things
that happen to some children are so deep and the
memories aren't all was bitter sweet. The feeling of
being totally out of control and being beaten up.

The blood that was shed over nothing and the scares that
remain in my heart and the images that can't simply
stop or be taken back.

These things remain in my heart and my head forever
thanks to one miserable old man and that man was my father
and let no other man that over again. The past has come
full circle and it's time to stop.

THE END.

I Can't Stop

I can't stop thinking of you, I can't stop dreaming of you.
My heart and my head are totally over heels in love with you.
And I just can't sleep.

It hurts me when were apart
And I can't stop thinking of you
And stop the romance in our life time.

You are my every waking moment.
You are my every waking thought
Through our day and into the night.

And together we can accomplish anything,
Because our love is strong and we both believe.

MY HAPPINESS

Every morning when I awake
I only have thoughts of you.
My life would surely have a big hole in it
Without you to fill it.
You're all ways in my mind being tossed around.
You're always in my heart to keep me strong.
You are my every waking thought.
You are my pations, you are my light, you are all mine.
I don't know exactly what I did in my life time,
But I'm very glad I did it.
I'm happiest with you be my side
Because there is no sacrifice.
My life is complete and now I can sleep.

Open heart

In my heart of hearts, in the deepest part of my soul I've searched the world from end to end in my mind just to find that special someone. Through the years of expectation, though the years of wondering, through the men I've been with, just was never you. My heart will remain empty, my mind to continue for the search for the one man to call my own. The time I've wasted looking and wondering if my life was ever going to be mine. The man of my dreams he will always remain till this one day I find him and we can become one. My long search is finally over for I finally found him, he's perfect in every way as my dreams have predicted and all thanks to you. My heart is now full and I'm blessed each and every day that I have you. You are my world you are my life and I never want to change a thing.

TOGETHER FOREVER

I hurt when you hurt, I'm sad when your sad, I cry when you cry.
But when you and I are together nothing else matters.
We have become one in this life time together.
You have this way of making me laugh and forget about the past.
You have this way of always making my day better.
My life had all ways felt so incomplete and so alone till that one faithful day I found you.
You've opened my eyes to see, and opened my heart to feel, and I thank-you for that.
I thank you for being mine in this life and beyond.

FORGIVENESS

Some times in the darkest part of our minds
Things that have happened in the past come back in time.
Your mind is a very powerfull drug that
Sometimes won't shut down.

The things we remember but try to forget
Because the pain of the past is so great.
The horrible things that happen
To some children are so deep
And the memories aren't all was bitter sweet.
The feeling of being totally out of control
And being beaten up.

The blood that was shed over nothing
And the scares that remain in my heart
And the Images that can't simply stop
Or be taken back.

These things remain in my heart and my head forever
Thanks to one miserable old man
And that man was my father
And let no other man that over again.
The past has come full circle and it's time to stop.

THE END

My Emptiness

It feels like it's been forever in a life time all though
in reality it's only been two days. I hate it when were
apart. My days and nights are so empty without you.

The hours and minutes with in my mind just stand
still when you're not around. My life without you in it
just seems so difficult and like unwound twine. The
longing I have when were not together is pain that
I simply can't ignore.

I can't wait for your arms to be wrapped around me,
I can't wait for our lips to touch again. My heart is yours
now and forever the way that it was all ways meant to be.
Our lives enter twined together for all time. You only get
lucky in love this much once in a life time and this is
ours to life out for all time.

I'm happiest with you by my side.

LONELY

Life is to short and
precious to take for
granted. My children are
my Life my Feeling and
my Pain are real, sometimes
in Life things happen
that are out of our control.
Sometime maybe things
in life happen for a
reason. Things in Life
sometimes are hard to
understand or explain
But through my pain
and heartbreak I have
My children and they will always
be there to keep me
strong. My words that I
write in my poetry of
Life is sometimes just
a way of thought and
Feelings of mine to
true to remain me
alone in time. for now
I life for today and
not tomorrow because
it may not be here for
me my life may never
Be the same for now I stand
alone in fear and darkness.

My Sorrow

Roses are Red Violets are
Blue my Heart is breaking
Because of you. All the
mistakes I've made. All
the sacrifices that
remain. My Heart is
truly breaking. How
could you do Such mean
and deceitful things,
I Lost my way in
this time and I will
find the strength I
need to carry on with in
myself. my Heart
is truly Breaking over
the things that you
made me do and for the thoughts
that remain in my head
and weight on my heart
my tears run down my
face every time I think
of it.

MY PAIN

Have you ever been stolen from
Have you ever had something taken.
Have you ever felt lost and alone
Have you ever been scared and lost
Have you ever asked for help and
there's no one there.
Have you lost all hope and fear
Runs your life.
Have you lost everything that
matters and no one cares
Does the loneliness within
your heart get difficult to bare
I know of all these things
because I are there, lost,
alone and scared. no one
chooses to help me they all
turn away. The Fight that is
left is my cross to bare and
Fight I shall I will not stop
I would let my past dictate
My future no matter what.

ROSES

Roses are Red Violets are
Blue My Heart is truly
Braking over the things about
you. I thought you were
good only to find that you
weren't the one. Your life is
so full of Evil your mind
and heart are both so
unkind. The things that you've
done are scary to me. The
truth of it all is all about
to come to an end. All I have
left is the faith in myself.
for everything else that I have
lost. I hope the world that
we live in can see you for
all you're worth. your cruel
ways that you have will come
to an end then maybe I
can life again.

STRENGTH

The thoughts in my mind now
after everything that's gone wrong.
The feelings in my heart
that use to be so strong
The love we once shared
is now gone. My Life as I
once new it is no more the
only emotion that is now
is lose and anger for
that's All I have now my
Life is over. thanks to
you I'll remain strong for
that's all that I am.

SADNESS

The sadness I feel so deep
with in my heart The pain
of the thought of never being
or seeing you again The
anger and Sad thoughts that
sit in my mind The anger
of what's Happened imbedded
into my soul The great loss
I have now I wish would
just go.

CRAZY

My Heart is Breaking over the
lose my Heart is Heavy
Because of that. My mind
is going crazy with the
thoughts that control my
Brain. My anger that I
feel the pain that is so
great I sometimes wonder
if I will ever get my life
Back The pain to slowly
heal and the past is forgot.

THINGS CHANGE

The things I have Lost
can not be found.
The feelings I once had
are now all gone.
By a single man in a
Single moment have you
ever had your life turned
upside down. Have you
ever lost everything by
the hand of another
Have you ever felt. So
lost and alone This is me
I once had everything
But one day evil stepped
in and now I have nothing.

MY PAIN

Have you ever been stolen from
Have you ever had something taken
Have you ever felt lost and alone
Have you ever been scared and lost
Have you ever asked for help and
there's no one there.
Have you lost all hope and fear
Runs your life.
Have you lost everything that
matters and no one cares
Does the loneliness within
your heart get difficult to bare
I know of all these things
because I are there, lost,
alone and scared. no one
chooses to help me they all
turn away. The Fight that is
left is my cross to bare and
Fight I shall I will not stop
I would let my past dictate
My future no matter what.

CONGRATULATIONS

In life everyone and everybody has a side that can be creative.
In life many people have more then some.
I life there are many choices to be made.
In life there are many regrets and sometimes lots of let downs.

But all in all to those of you that take that chance, that have that
one simple thought I congratulate each and everyone.

Keep up the good work whether be happy or be sad. It's your
emotions that count when you write them down.
good luck to you all in your writing and in your life.
I sincerely bless each and everyone.

Thank-you . . .

DON'T LOOK

I once lived next door to an old man who always left his house at a quarter to eight each and every day. I don't know where he went but he always came back one hour later at nine o'clock precisely. As I would watch him through my bedroom window I wondered where he goes at the same time each and every day. I would watch him get into his car each day but were he went nobody new. As I watched him drive away I thought to myself I know nothing of this man not his name, or whom he knew.

I do know that he's an old man that lives across the street from me and that he always leaves his house the same time of day. He was a very handsome man and had a head of white hair and stood about six feet tall, but I never say anybody stop by for a visit which I thought to be quite weird. I've watched this man come and go each end every day until today when curiosity got the best of me. The next morning when I saw him leave I ran down the stairs and out the front door. I did not have much time to break in to his house and see, as I stood there in his living room I saw many pictures upon his walls, they were pictures of an older woman probably around the old man's age early sixties with small children sitting upon their knee. I was starting to feel a bit uneasy for breaking in so I quickly left and hoped I didn't leave any evidence of myself behind.

I ran back to my house and up to my room laid down on my bed and decided what to do next. I thought about it and decided to follow him the next day. That morning when I awoke I got myself dressed and out the front door I went. As I hid in the bush waiting for him to leave I was feeling a bit scared because what if he can see me. I took a deep breath and off I went. As I was following him he turned down this old dirt road just outside of town I slowed down to make sure to stay out of site. I was starting to sweat and shake a bit for just at the thought of getting caught, just then the old man pulled over near this old run down house. I pulled over just before that and hope that he can't see me or I'm dead meat. I watched him as he got out of his car and went into the house, so I got out of my car and hide in the bush.

As I waited there I saw the upstairs light turn on then talking and stumbling about but not soon after the man came back out. He got into his car and left just like that. I needed to know who was in there so I slowly went over and opened the door. As I went in I could someone speaking out so I went up the stairs quietly for they were squeaking. I went into the room where I heard a voice and on the be there was an old lady sitting upright. She said with a start 'o my you have given me such a freight 'I said hi to her and sorry for the scare but I was just really curious to as who was just here. The old woman looked at me and smiled and said 'o my dear that was my son he comes by to see me two times a week.' I really started to feel silly as I explained to her what I was doing, the old woman just looked at me and laughed. I left the house that day feeling better about the old man there was no mystery just two good friends and that's what family is. No more Mystery no more wondering just an end.

My Monster Under My Bed

I often feel that I have spent my entire life in the fear of something that happened to me when I was young. That is what created the monster under my bed.

The fears and wants that took hold of my head and my heart. The fears that were instilled in me that just would not go away.

The monster under my bed stayed to scare me and keep me from living day to day. After all those years the monster has left thanks to my man in my life. He has believed in me, and now that he is here with me my fears are slowly going away.

The man of my dreams, the man I love has taken a stand to protect me. The monster under my bed is now gone and just true love is what remains. The one thing that I could never do on my own ever again and I thank-you my love for the understanding and simply believing in me. Now I am strong with you by my side I need not ever fear again to stand alone.

Freedom is now here at last the monster under my bed is gone.

MIND OF MADNESS

As the sun began to rise over the mountains I hear the birds
outside my window. As I watched
them fly high up into the sky, the noises they made echoed in my head.
The birds never used to bother me
so much till that one fateful day, when I was young.
My father took me by the hand and showed me
how evil the birds have become. They came down all at once
and pecked at me until blood came
running down my face.

My father sat and watched and never once reached out his hand to help.
Since that day I've been in my house
watching the birds fly by and pecking at my window as to say come
back. I sit and wonder that if on that faith full day
that my father had a plan of my death.
I can't escape my past, I can't forget, I
can't get the birds out of my head.

I can't carry on one more day, so I must put this to rest. As I open my
window,
I say to you all take me now as
I fall, release me from my past, no more birds in my head.
I have finally come to rest. The birds of my
past die with me, peace at last.

AT THE BEACH

I love the ocean, I love the sea especially when
it's just you and me.

One little baby rock sitting on the beach looking
really sad maybe he needs to be a seat.

There are so many rocks on the beach some really
big and some not. I wonder what wonders they hold
underneath.

Push, push, push the rock, roll it over and lets take
a look. Crabs are crawling underneath with squishy
worms moving by my feet.

The water is getting cold now as the sun begins to
set over the water and behind the mountains.

But mom says that we can come back tomorrow again
to have some more fun in the sun.

Author Notes Helen Smith

ATTRACTION . . . .

Today was a day like no other recent day I've ever had. My friend Helen and I were out for lunch at this new restaurant called the Shato Gardens, it was just down the street from where I lived it had a good reputation for its food so we figured we'd go try it out. As we were about to order our food I looked up and saw this man sitting at the table across from us. I swear he was the most gorgeous looking man that I've seen in a very long time, I found it hard to stop looking at him. He stood at about six foot two and had medium blond hair that just touched his shoulders, and his eyes were like looking into clear blue water; I found him to be was just breathtaking. My friend Helen noticed me staring across the room and finally kicked me under the table "Karoline," Helen said "what are you looking at"? oh, 'I'm sorry" Karoline I replied, I was just day dreaming.' As we finished our lunch about to leave I looked up and saw him coming towards my direction I started to feel Faint I thought is he coming over to talk to me. Before I knew it he was standing in front of me all six feet of him. He came over and said "I hope you don't fine me rude but I saw you looking at me, is there something I can do for you?. "oh No" I replied quickly". Allow me to introduce myself my name is Samuel, I am new here in your fare city and don't know many people may I suggest to you that maybe you could show me around ". I just sat there thinking that this couldn't be happening to me he's gorgeous and he had a wonderful accent and was very soft spoken. It took me a minute to catch my breath before replying "yes that would be nice" As I took a napkin to write my number upon it he leaned down towards me and softly took my hand in his and kissed it. I swear that I almost fell of my chair." till later then" he said and I just shook my head up and down and said "good-bye" Karoline, Helen said "are you nuts he could be a serial killer or something and you give him your phone number." "Don't be stupid he seems very nice and he's cute to boot" replied Karoline. Helen looks at her with miss belief of what she had said As we got up and ready to pay the bill we left the restaurant and went home "I'll talk to you later Helen don't worry so much Samuel probable won't even call" but down deep inside I hoped that he would.

When I got home the first thing I did was have a cold shower for some reason I just couldn't get him out of my head I started to think to myself are you really that hard up or just infatuated by the thought of the whole thing, I guess that time would tell. The next evening it was a Friday the phone rang it was Samuel he asked me to go to the movies

With him tonight, of course I said yes. We were going to see Never say forever. I went to my closet to find something to wear I wanted to look perfect, I must have tried on everything I owned but I just couldn't decide finally I found it my spaghetti strap red dress it came up just above my knees and it was a tight fit to show off my figure it was perfect. As a knock at my door happened I took a deep breath "it must be him" I said" as I smiled to myself as I went to open the door and there he was dressed in a dark blue suit and he had red roses in his right hand. I invited him in as he gave me the roses he said" I guess I bought the right flowers they go with the pretty dress you're wearing. I replied "thank-you" "shall we go then" Samuel asked in a low but strong voice "yes I'm ready. When we were at the movie he held my hand so very tenderly it was nice. After the movie I suggested that I could take him sightseeing around the city Samuel expressed that it was a wonderful idea. Later that evening we went back to his hotel room I was a bit nerves to say the least because I haven't had sex with anyone in a very long time, actually I've only had sex once in my live. Samuel poured us a glass of red wine and we sat together on the sofa till about two in the morning talking about everything and anything that came to our minds. I found him to be a very easy person to talk to about my thoughts and feelings these days it's hard to find someone to listen to you. I found it very refreshing I was starting to feel a bit tipsy from the wine so I wanted to lay down, Samuel took my hand and led me to his bedroom. He slowly began to unzip my dress and slide it down over my shoulders, I was so drunk that I didn't fight it, he dropped my dress to the floor as it landed around my feet. As he began to undo my bra, his lips followed slowly down to my breasts as he held my hands to my sides. He slowly started removing his clothing dropping them to the floor, I had surrendered my whole body and soul to him, we made love all night it was as if we became one person it was like the first time for both of us he was like a child exploring every part of my body, as he suckled my breasts his mouth and soft lips were kissing me all the way down to my inner thigh, I gasped and arched my back in excitement as he began to bite and nibble my thigh I thought that I was going to bleed. But pleasure is more powerful than any pain as you could imagine it was wonderful.

As the sun began to rise by the time I awoke Samuel had already left there was a note place upon his pillow that read" with sweet sorrow I must leave and I'll see you tomorrow". I crawled myself from his bed and had a cool shower, got dressed and left with wonderful thoughts of that evening, for I couldn't wait see him again. My life is bound to be wonderful that is if I can keep him.

THE END

AT THE BEACH

These short stories are
dedicated to my four children
that helped to inspire me.
Lance, Taylor, Cameron
Karoline.

Written by Helen Smith.

I love the ocean, I love the sea
especially when it's just my mom
and me.

One little baby rock sitting on the beach, but there is a bigger one over there or maybe not.

I wonder what's underneath,
mom come and help me push
the rock, Cameron come and take
a look

Push, push, push the rock roll
it over and see the wonders
underneath.

Crabs are crawling on the beach
and squishy worms are moving
beneath my feet.

The water is getting very cold
now as the sun begins to set,
over the water at the beach.

But we can come back tomorrow
Cameron just you and me to have
more fun among the rocks, under
the warm sun by the ocean and the
sea. It's time for bed for you and for me.

THE END . . .

SPIDER LEGS . . .

These short stories are
dedicated to my four
beautiful children that
helped to inspire me . . .
Lance, Taylor, Cameron
Karoline

Written by Helen Smith.

Eight little spider legs crawling
across my floor one fell off then
it wasn't there no more.

Seven little spider legs crawling
up my wall one fell off and got
stuck in a hole.

Six little spider legs crawling
across the table one fell off
and landed in my soup.

Five little spider legs crawling
across my bed one leg got stuck
and got ripped off.

Four little spider legs hanging
in the wind one leg blew away then
there were three.

Three little spider legs fighting
to stay on, one fell off then two
remained.

Two little spider legs left to stand
alone, one leg falls off to make
it a lonely one.

One little spider leg left by himself
so he made a great wish and they
all came back. again.

Eight little spider legs together
once again, crawling up his web
and back again.

THE END . . . .

Printed in the United States
By Bookmasters